WOUNDED LIVES
WOUNDED HEALERS

How to Break FREE from Emotional Pain
to bring Balance back into your Life

By ESTHER AUSTIN

Printed by The Printing House
Published by Esther Austin Global Publishing
Copyright@ Esther Austin Global Publishing

Book cover designed by Cameron Austin-Buah
Photograph taken by David Connelly
http://www.davidcphotography.uk

TABLE OF CONTENTS

ENDORSEMENTS

Wounded Lives, Wounded Healers is an important book for our times. It helps the reader through the voices and lives of others to find hope and sanctuary in moving beyond the emotional pain and trauma to a life of greater joy and freedom. It's one for your book collection.

Jackee Holder Author, Coach and Speaker (UK)

This book will undoubtedly touch many in more ways than is fathomable, allowing you to tap into your emotions, to face those emotions and release them. If you want to confront yourself, unshackle your fears and break free of your limitations, then this is a MUST read.

Shirley-Ann Hunte, Business Professional

Wounded Lives, Wounded Healers
Like ballet dancers, toes pointed on
the razor blades of our lives
we tiptoe along the darkened corridors
of broken promises and guilt's perceptive dirty shame
where laughter no longer breathes life into the smile
and where pain's toxic residue resides
littered on the carpet of our lives.

The corridors of faith are dim with the ashes of the fallen
of those who could not find their strength
nor conviction to believe in who they truly are
or who chose not to stand within the
columns of their own power
their essence no longer stirs nor mingles with the living
their cries now mere whispers within the walls
of shame, guilt, fear, doubt and obligation
smeared on the bed of their own pain.

Like travellers on a pilgrimage this world of
pain becomes the existence of many
the weight and illusion of such lies
becoming their very existence.
yet for those who catch a glimpse of the universal truth
and who now know how to walk on the shoulders of pain
the playground of life's learning adventure
they find HOPE and discover LOVE
because only the truth can set us free

And truth can only be found in the arms of love

Esther Austin

DEDICATION

Breast Cancer Support Centres

I dedicate this book to my Late sister Deborah Austin who died in 2006 from Breast Cancer.

My sister touched the lives of so many people when she was alive. The Haven was an organisation who my sister said did so much for her in her final days therefore I will be dedicating proceeds from the book to The Haven.

The Haven supports people with breast cancer. They provide emotional support, complementary therapies, information, advice and classes designed to help each person with their own personal challenges of living with or beyond breast cancer. Their services are free of charge. www.thehaven.org.uk

I also dedicate this book to YOU the reader, to anyone and everyone who has ever walked with pain and who has the courage to gently face it in order to heal and transform and find peace.

INTRODUCTION

I wanted to weave a tapestry of experiences, wisdom, guidance and advice through this book wanting to get in-depth insight from experts, practitioners, teachers and educators in order to draw out rich and insightful wisdom and experiences of their journey. I wanted to hear where they personally came from, their pain, frustrations and their own process of facing, dealing with and then transforming their own emotional baggage and how they used those experiences to help others. I wanted to hear their "How to's." I believe we can learn better through the stories and experiences of others, as it becomes a way we can relate to each other. By knowing that someone has gone through a similar experience to ours helps support us on our own journey.

I hope this book will empower you to look at your life through the telescope of internal self inquiry giving you the opportunity to find an answer to life beyond your personal limitations. I hope you get the chance to explore who you truly are and to face your shadow side, a side which many shy away from because it's not a place we often visit. We've got used to living behind our masks and keeping secrets. Therefore, the intention of this book is to support you in finding your own truth through the process of finding balance within your life.

I also hope this book will open up a doorway within yourself which you can step into and embrace life on a level that exceeds your own dreams, limitations and expectations. A life where every moment can become "Soul-filled" and where the platform of love becomes your throne to build upon, create, to dream from and then to be able to reach inside your own Pandora's box of internal wealth, into your own pot-pourri of tools, gifts, talents to discover who you truly are. It is my intention that the information in this book will open many doorways for you to experience the best of love, in your intimate, soul-mate relationships, friendships and generally the best that life can offer you. But first you must believe you are deserving to have such experiences and then for you to make that change within yourself to find out what is blocking you, what pain or emotional "stuff" has you chained.

**An Important Principle for
Establishing Balance in Your Life**

There is an important principle around balance that I would like to share before commencing with this book, because as with the experience of pain and emotional wounding there is the balance of setting ourselves free. This principle integrates the components of the two sides of life but we often do not recognise that our focus is usually on the negative experiences and our pain from those which we have not resolved, transformed or healed. Therefore, bringing balance is the experience of everything, the experience that brings about wholeness and a totality of who we are whilst also embracing our experiences of brokenness and wounding. Without balance in life there can be no stability, harmony, unity etc.

So therefore if there is light there must be darkness, if there is up there is also down, backwards and forwards, happy days, down days, love and hate. With everything there are always opposite ends of any spectrum.

To help reference the word BALANCE we must look at its opposite UNBALANCE because this is where many people live, in the pain and wounding of being unbalanced.

I googled the word Unbalance "to upset or disturb the equilibrium of (i.e a situation or person's state of mind)". So being in a state of unbalance brings about disturbance and even chaos within oneself, or within a system of things. Yet chaos can also be a good thing because from the rumblings of that place renewal, change, rebirth and transformation begin to take place leading to a place of balance. This process brings about an awareness of the pain, of the dysfunction, of the upset, of our wounding yet it also brings about an awareness of the possibility that something better can be experienced and moved into.

So what balance does is it brings us back into who we truly. It gives us the chance to once again re-connect with our truth and to accept that we have these myriad of experiences in order to understand everything. To bring balance from that place of wounding is to go on a journey of healing and transformation using whatever tools, modalities and techniques that resonate with us. We are more than our pain and our wounding. We are also love, abundance, acceptance, happiness, joy and much more…...

"It's better to be unhappy alone than unhappy with someone."

Marilyn Monroe

WITH BALANCE
I MAINTAIN WHOLENESS

CHAPTER ONE – THE WOUNDED HEALER

Wounded Healer is a term created by psychologist Carl Jung. The idea states that an analyst is compelled to treat patients because the analyst himself is "wounded". The idea may have Greek mythology origins. Research has shown that 73.9% of counsellors and psychotherapists have experienced one or more wounding experiences leading to career choice.

As an example, of the "wounded healer phenomenon" between an analyst and his/her analysed:

- The analyst is consciously aware of his own personal wounds. These wounds may be activated in certain situations especially if his analysed wounds are similar to his own.[1]

- The analysed wounds affect the wounds of the analyst. The analyst either consciously or unconsciously passes this awareness back to his analysed, causing an unconscious relationship to take place between analyst and analysed.[2]

   http://en.wikipedia.org/wiki/Wounded_healer

I write this book from a place where I am now neither victim nor martyr but from a place of being a survivor. I share some of my story within these pages but not all, as for me the past now needs to remain in the past, well for those parts which I have healed. Yet what I choose to share with you is simply to support you and hopefully give you an insight into how you too can come through the other side.

By journeying through this book along with the messages shared by other practitioners, the collaborative experiences show that the Soul is indeed an incredible piece of engineering and that humanity in its darkest moments can always find the will, the way, the tenacity and determination to stand on the shoulders of pain and rise like a phoenix from the ashes. Yet in order to rise from a place of brokenness into a stronger place, healing of the mind, body and soul must be part of that journey so we can stand confident and enriched within our own totality and wholeness with the tale of our journey but not limited nor defined by the wounds of our journey.

Hence that is why life is called a journey because of its precarious and sometimes tenuous meanderings, its ups and downs, its highs and lows. Sometimes the unpredictability of this journey keeps us locked in the realm of fear, not wanting to face the unknown nor step outside our comfort zones. Other times life can feel as if we're on a trajectory of flow swaying us from one place to the next. Yet whatever road we choose on a subconscious level and however we choose to travel it, the outcome is usually for our greater good, improved learning and growth which therefore becomes a trajectory towards our destiny.

The more I have journeyed with my own personal self-mastery is the more I realise there is so much more of who we are that we do not allow ourselves to be, simply because we choose often unconsciously to hold onto so much "stuff or baggage" and also because of fear. At times we are not even aware we are holding onto anything as it becomes a load which we harness to our backs until it becomes such a part of us that it's often hard to put down because it feels comfortable and there is no distinction between us and our pain.

There are many reasons why we carry emotional baggage. The baggage comes from many places and experiences and if you believe in past lives, it comes from those places as well as generational, cultural and traditional places.

It has taken me a while to fully step into that place of power within myself as I had to take an up-close and personal journey with Esther to get to where I am now. Once I recognised there was more to me I had to go on a journey to understand what was blocking me from stepping into my greatness. On a more basic level a lot of what was showing up externally in my world was a result of my internal dialogue with feelings of doubt, feeling unloved and undeserving. A lot of this "stuff" was because of past emotional wounds and pain that were still unresolved.

Les Brown, the American Motivational Speaker once said "most people fail in life not because they aim too high and miss but most people fail in life because they aim too low and hit."

How we learn to respond to life's situations is key and what we choose to do with them and what tools, techniques and resources we have around us to support us helps the healing process. The most powerful thing I have learned personally when dealing with pain is to use it as a stepping stone and not let it stagnate within as this only causes illness and dis-ease within the body, which I have experienced, an indicator that I needed to deal with something in my life.

Recently, I've been reflecting on some of my personal challenges and after listening to "The Science of Getting Rich by Bob Proctor, Dr Michael Beckwith and Jack Canfield" in one of the chapters Bob Proctor says "we have small challenges, we have small blessings. We have big challenges, we have big blessings, that's just life and everything just is." That really helped me put my situation and experiences more into perspective.

I often get asked "What determines someone's response or reaction to challenges, tragedy, pain? Why would one person internalise a situation one way and climb on the shoulders of pain whilst another looses hope and the will-power to keep going? For me there are no definitive answers, I just believe that whatever pain anyone carries, wherever anyone has been in their lives that that place can be touched through the process of love, patience, insight, some form of therapy and it can be transformed and healed.

This does not mean that the journey of transformation and healing will be a smooth path. It generally gets rockier and more painful before things get better. You may feel vulnerable and exposed because you no longer recognise who you are, your identity is challenged which then affects your perception of who you are and your role in the world. Yet the one thing which is guaranteed in life is change and death. Change is inevitable and for me change means transformation and transformation means healing and healing brings balance.

CHAPTER TWO – MY JOURNEY

My journey has been an eclectic roller coaster of painful emotional experiences, incredible challenges, great opportunities and successes. The times when I felt that life was too much to handle, I would somehow find an inner strength to draw on. Part of that was a discipline I adopted of exercise, listening to music, praying and meditating.

Wounded Lives, Wounded Healers captures so much of who I am and my journey and therefore informs the work I do with my clients. I am an Intuitive Healer and I feel the below excerpt really sums up my own journey with my own woundedness and now I am a healer.

'The 'wounded healer' theory (Guggenbuhl - Craig 1971; Rippere and Williams 1985). says that the pain of the healer is the source of their power to heal others and that the healer's own experiences form the foundations of their empathy with clients and their 'wounds'. The theory goes on to say that there is a danger of the healer being sacrificed by his or her 'wounds' being exacerbated by the demands of those being helped. I like the idea of the therapist's pain being used to help others. After all, who better to understand difficulties than a person who understands them from his or her own frame of reference?'

A few years ago I worked with a client who was going through depression. As I conducted a session of Hypno-analysis and Regression therapy I suddenly recognised her experience within my own. It then dawned on me that many of my clients' experiences reflected an aspect of my experience. When this client described her sense of hopelessness and isolation I was able to reference back to those times when I felt this way. Up until this moment with this client I had never associated myself with the experience of depression.

My journey, like many, has been an eclectic mix of many experiences. I've been homeless briefly, experienced emotional abuse, handed over my personal power until I found myself justifying basic human freedoms such as why I wanted to wash my hair, to cook, being told to discipline myself when I wanted to go to the toilet, down to explaining why I wanted to watch a certain program on TV. Other times the TV would be turned off and taken out of the room as I watched it. I handed over my personal power so much that I often found myself walking the streets late at night crying because I needed to find my space and hold onto my sanity and peace. However there was always that warrior spirit in me which said "down but not out." Crazier moments were when I found myself justifying why I wanted to bake a cake, or cook pancakes, or the times where I would hoover for hours on end so when my ex came home he would see the lines on the carpet which proved I had tidied up. My marriage at the time felt as if I was constantly going into emotional battle and I was always on emotional alert to constant criticism and judgement. Yet through it all I wrote four books, I was awarded a Skillset Millennium Award which involved training with The BBC and Skillset to set up a media project. I created a website called Caribbean Woman – Focus in the Community where I interviewed inspirational women from the Caribbean about their lives. Many times during the training I took my children along with me because I had no-one to leave them with. I had a dream and I was going to fulfil that dream no matter what it took. My determination and dedication to succeed meant that I was asked by Skillset and the BBC (who had partnered with Skillset on this project) to speak at the Award Ceremony to launch the first stages of the project and what an honour that was because after all I had been through, standing on stage talking to over 200 people at the BBC, I felt as if I had been handed my own personal Oscar. Best of all my children came with me to the Launch and went through all the media packs and took my profile out and unbeknown to me, handed my profile out to everyone in the room and for that they got a standing ovation from the crowd after my talk. That was really a proud moment for me because they had inspired me to keep going and I had inspired them in some way to do what they did.

Another pivotal point in my life was in August 2005 when my younger sister found out breast cancer had come back. That battle lasted until November 2006 when she died. My sister was my best friend and that experience took me on a very intense and deep spiritual journey. One which left me in a much stronger place where I learned so much about handling pain on every level. After that experience my intuitive abilities and healing capabilities opened up even more. I believe this was because I had experienced so much pain with my sister's experience that this pushed me to the very limits of every emotional capacity from love, compassion, hope, regret, vulnerability, hopelessness etc.

Therefore wanting to give something back, I undertook a charity challenge to raise money for The Haven, a charity who supported my sister while she was sick. I trekked the Inca Trail in Peru. Even after much training, I ended up walking with a walking stick at the back of the group with a group of doctors and a Sherpa because on day four of the trip my legs gave out and I had to be carried back to base because I could not walk. My legs would shake as if I had Parkinson's Disease and then I would loose all sense of feeling in them. Interestingly the first time this happened I remember having a vision flash through me of my late sister walking with a zimmerframe as in the last few months of her life she had become incredibly weak. So on a subconscious level I probably wanted to experience the pain she went through as some sort of cathartic experience. So for the next 6 days of my charity trek I had to be topped up with injections to help stabilise my leg and use a walking stick. A days trek would often take me an extra two or three hours but I always got back to base in the end, because this was a journey I knew I had to take.

There have been many other painful and challenging moments but the one thing that kept me going was my vision that one-day I knew I would be successful enough to have my own business and be able to reach out and transform lives and knowing that my experiences would feed into this process on a profound level.

I've gone without food, I've worked through the day and night to fulfil my dream, I've been homeless briefly. I've had to walk for hours on end to get to a meeting because I had no money, sat huddled up in a freezing cold room without heat working on my dream (I needed heat to be available when my children got home from school because otherwise I couldn't afford to keep it on).

Yet I now understand why I had to have those experiences and they are just the tip of the iceberg. I now know that they have made me who I am in order to do the work I do. Yet first and foremost I had to do a lot of work on myself and I continue to do so. I share below some of the things that have kept me sane through life's challenges.

Being a very strong Intuitive Healer and Intuitive Reader means clients who come to see me, are often very broken yet I feel blessed and privileged that I can resonate with them on a level where I can reach into their darkest and most secret of spaces. I am gifted at being able to see, sense and feel what is going on inside a persons body on an emotional, spiritual, physical and psychological level. My experiences have empowered me to be exceptionally sensitive and empathetic to others because I have been through so much pain myself.

TIPS, TOOLS AND RECOMMENDATIONS

- Find a quiet spot and make it yours.

- Listen to music, sing, dance, exercise.

- Find someone you trust and can talk to because when we internalise our pain it doesn't go away, it just resides in the background and shows up in other ways.

- Meditate or pray - or if you don't do either then focus on your breathing because this helps to calm the mind.

- Journal because it's a cathartic release.

- Cuddle your pet if you have one. Animals play a huge part in a person's healing process because intuitively they feel how you are feeling and their presence offers calm and peace.

- Play like a child – this helps get rid of any inhibitions.

- **Hugs and Cuddles:** The physical effect of touch encourages increased blood flow which brings fresh nutrients to the surface of the skin, giving it a natural glow.

- **Holistic Healing:** If you need more in-depth support, try Life-coaching, Intuitive Healing, Reiki, Massage and/or any other energy healing work. These modalities work on a Mind, Body and Soul level treating the whole person and not just the symptom.

"You are the master of your destiny. You can influence, direct and control your own environment. You can make your life what you want it to be."

Napoleon Hill, *Think and Grow Rich*

Image taken by Ray Paulden, from Creative Eye
http://www.creative-eye.org

CHAPTER THREE – WHO AM I?

How many times have you allowed your voice to be silenced? Through obligation and self-denial. Life is like being on stage. Consciously or unconsciously we choose the characters we portray and play. We can be the drama queens of our own experiences or we can be the powerful orator, strong in stance, strong in conviction, strong in expressing our inner desires, wishes and dreams. Yet as we journey through life we often transition from one character into another, depending on how we perceive, interpret and internalize our emotional experiences and therefore who we become as a result of them.

This may be the first time where you are taking the time to really look at your life, how you are feeling, and what you really want. Maybe your pain is so intense that you are now looking for ways of dealing with it asking yourself questions such Who am I? How am I feeling? How can I deal with this emotional tiredness and pain? So how does the possibility of putting YOU first feel? Do you even know who YOU are anymore underneath the rubble of wounds and pain?

Then there are the questions of "Where do I go to put me back together? How do I start this personal transformational journey? Who do I trust to support me? And more importantly how do I recognize what this pain is doing to me?

Activity:

Below are some key words which you may identify with. Do you recognise yourself in any of them?

Are you feeling: Empty, Confused, Lonely, Frustrated, Disillusioned, Stagnant, Resentful, Angry, Feeling a Failure, Unworthy, Emotionally Exhausted, Unloved,

Isolated, Victimised, Not listened to, Undermined and Undervalued, Not feeling good enough, Not being able to see the light at the end of the tunnel, Constantly tired.

If you recognise yourself in the above then the next question is:

ARE YOU READY TO FACE YOURSELF IN THE MIRROR OF YOUR TRUTH?

It's not as scary as it sounds. Once you take that first step it becomes easier and whatever faces you back in your mirror of truth is simply saying to you, **I NEED HELP**. So without judgement you can take off the mask you have been wearing, possibly all your life and finally deal with **YOU**. You no longer have to pretend to be someone you are not. You can now stand in your truth, sometimes even feeling vulnerable. Hopefully you will find answers in the following chapters to help you gain a perspective on How to deal with your emotional baggage and pain.

CHAPTER FOUR – DEFINING EMOTIONS AND FEELINGS

Emotions control your thinking, behaviour and actions. Emotions affect your physical bodies as much as your body affects your feelings and thinking. People who ignore, dismiss, repress or just ventilate their emotions, are setting themselves up for physical illness. Emotions that are not felt and released but buried within the body or in the aura can cause serious illness, including cancer, arthritis, and many types of chronic illnesses. Negative emotions such as fear, anxiety, negativity, frustration and depression cause chemical reactions in your body that are very different from the chemicals released when you feel positive emotions such as happy, content, loved, accepted.

Our belief systems underlie much of our behaviour and is usually our filter system which interprets what we see and hear therefore affecting how we behave in our daily lives. Also belief systems are not a truth in themselves, they are just systems of what we tell ourselves or what we have internalised from what we have been told throughout our lives. If you have grown up being told that you are ugly, then your subconscious takes it to be true.

There are many other elements that affect our lives, including past lives and the core issues we come into this life for resolution, but our belief systems in this life have a major effect on what we think and do. It takes a lot of work to look at yourself and identify the beliefs that are affecting your life in a negative manner. However, knowing your beliefs will give you a sound basis for emotional freedom. I believe that it's wise to deal with belief systems before dealing with the identification and release of emotions. First things first!

The only person who can change what you feel is you. A new relationship, a new house, a new car, a new job, these things can momentarily distract you from your feelings, but no other person, no material possession, no activity can remove, release, or change how you feel. Our feelings remain within us until we release them.

There are only two basic emotions that we all experience, love and fear. All other emotions are variations of these two emotions. Thoughts and behaviour come from either a place of love, or a place of fear. Anxiety, anger, control, sadness, depression, inadequacy, confusion, hurt, lonely, guilt, shame, these are all fear-based emotions. Emotions such as joy, happiness, caring, trust, compassion, truth, contentment, satisfaction, these are love-based emotions.

Emotions have a direct effect on how our bodies work. Fear-based emotions stimulate the release of one set of chemicals while love-based emotions release a different set of chemicals. If the fear-based emotions are long-term or chronic they damage the chemical systems, the immune system, the endocrine system and every other system in your body. Our immune systems weaken and many serious illnesses set in. This relationship between emotions, thinking, and the body is being called Mind/ Body Medicine today.

You cannot change or control your emotions. You can learn how to be with them, living peacefully with them, transmuting them (which means releasing them), and you can manage them, but you cannot control them.

Think of the people who go along day after day seeming to function normally, and all of a sudden they will explode in anger at something that seems relatively trivial and harmless. That is one sign of someone who is trying to control or repress their emotions but their repressed emotions are leaking out.

The more anyone tries to control their emotions the more they resist control, and the more frightened people eventually become at what is seen to be a "loss of emotional control". It is a vicious circle.

People spend much time talking about how they feel. They talk and talk about their feelings but they don't feel their feelings. They intellectualise and analyse their feelings without feeling them.

People are afraid to really feel their feelings, afraid of losing control, afraid of the pain involved in feeling their emotions, of feeling the sense of loss or failure or whatever the emotion brings with it. People are afraid to cry. So much of life is about what you feel rather than what you think. Being strongly connected to your emotional life is essential to living a life with high energy and a sense of fulfilment and satisfaction.

It takes a lot of energy to keep emotions repressed and buried. If you keep emotions buried for a long period of time, you lower your overall vibrations, and lower vibrations lead to illness and an accelerated ageing process. Buried emotions create fatigue and depression. The following are some major symptoms of buried and repressed emotions.

- Fatigue

- Depression without an apparent cause

- Speaking of issues/interests rather than personal matters and feelings

- Pretending something doesn't matter when inside it does matter

- Rarely talking about your feelings

- Blowing up over minor incidents

- Walking around with a knot in your stomach or tightness in your throat

- Feeling your anger not at the time something happens but a few days later

- In relationships, focusing discussions on children/ money rather than talking about yourselves

- Troubled personal relationships with family, friends, acquaintances

- A lack of ambition or motivation

- Lethargic – who cares - attitude

- Difficulty accepting yourself and others

Emotional Release Exercise – Writing a Letter of Forgiveness

I use this exercise a lot in my Power of Forgiveness Workshops. Writing a letter to yourself and to others whether they are alive or have passed helps you release in a safe way anything you have suppressed and held onto. Often people wait for some form of resolution or forgiveness around painful experiences, yet this may never happen. Therefore in order to support you in moving on with your life and to release negativity that is trapped or suppressed emotionally within this is a great exercise to do where you pour out how you feel and have always felt about the situation which you are holding onto to. This process empowers you to release your pain. Then you can choose to send, bury or burn the letter whilst saying a mantra or prayer of forgiveness to yourself and to the other person involved.

Exercise

This poem by Marianne Williamson is one of my personal favourites. It says so much about how many people live their lives.

Read this poem two or three times, then get a pen and notepad and write down what you felt after reading the poem. What emotions did it bring up in you? Did you feel good about yourself after reading this? Did you have a moment of realisation?

Our Greatest Fear

It is our light not our darkness that most frightens us
Our deepest fear is not that we are inadequate
Our deepest fear is that we are powerful beyond measure.
It is our light not our darkness that most frightens us.
We ask ourselves, who am I to be brilliant, gorgeous,
talented and fabulous?

Actually, who are you not to be?
you are a child of God
your playing small does not serve the world.
there's nothing enlightened about shrinking so that other
people won't feel insecure around you.
we were born to make manifest the glory of
God that is within us.

It's not just in some of us; it's in everyone
and as we let our own light shine
we unconsciously give other people
permission to do the same.

As we are liberated from our own fear
our presence automatically liberates others.

Marianne Williamson

The Johari Windows Model

This article is about the cognitive psychology tool.

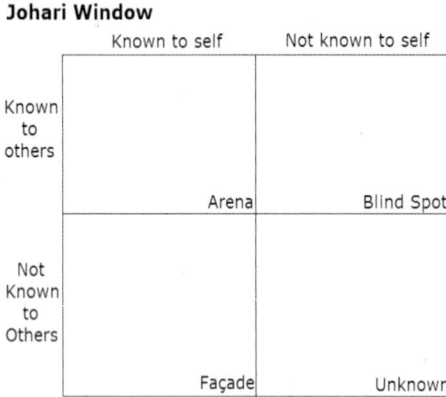

Johari Window

	Known to self	Not known to self
Known to others		
	Arena	Blind Spot
Not Known to Others		
	Façade	Unknown

Johari Window

Johari window as Venn diagram depicting intersection between a+) "Known to self" anda-) "Not known to self" on one hand, and on the other hand, b+) "Known to others" and b-) "Not known to others", with c showing the intersection containing four windows (or rooms)

The **Johari window** is a technique created in 1955 by two American psychologists, Joseph Luft (1916–2014) and Harrington Ingham (1914–1995) used to help people better understand their relationship with self and others.

When performing the exercise, subjects are given a list of 56 adjectives and pick five or six that they feel describe their own personality. Peers of the subject are then given the same list, and each pick five or six adjectives that describe the subject. These adjectives are then mapped onto a grid.

Charles Handy calls this concept the Johari House with four rooms. Room 1 is the part of ourselves that we see and others see. Room 2 is the aspects that others see but we are not aware of. Room 3 is the most mysterious room in that the unconscious or subconscious part of us is seen by neither ourselves nor others. Room 4 is our private space, which we know but keep from others.

Open or **Arena**: Adjectives that are selected by both the participant and his or her peers are placed into the **Open** or **Arena** quadrant. This quadrant represents traits of the subjects that both they and their peers are aware of.

Hidden or **Façade**: Adjectives selected only by subjects, but not by any of their peers, are placed into the **Hidden** or **Façade** quadrant, representing information about them their peers are unaware of. It is then up to the subject to disclose this information or not.

Blind Spot: Adjectives that are not selected by subjects but only by their peers are placed into the **Blind Spot** quadrant. These represent information that the subject is not aware of, but others are, and they can decide whether and how to inform the individual about these **"blind spots"**.

Unknown: Adjectives that were not selected by either subjects or their peers remain in the **Unknown** quadrant, representing the participant's behaviours or motives that were not recognized by anyone participating. This may be because they do not apply or because there is collective ignorance of the existence of these traits. One facet of interest in this area is our human potential. Our potential is unknown to us, and others.

A Johari window consists of the following 57 adjectives used as possible descriptions of the participant.[citation needed] - http://uk.wow.com/wiki/Johari_window?s_chn=55&s_pt=aolsem&v_t=aolsem

Able	Ambivert	Accepting
Adaptable	Bold	Calm
Caring	Cheerful	Clever
Congenial	Complex	Confident
Dependable	Dignified	Energetic
Extrovert	Friendly	Giving
Happy	Helpful	Idealistic
Independent	Ingenious	Intelligent
Introvert	Kind	Knowledgeable
Logical	Loving	Mature
Modest	Nervous	Observant
Optimistic	Organized	Patient
Powerful	Proud	Aggressive
Reflective	Relaxed	Religious
Responsive	Searching	Self-assertive
Self-conscious	Sensible	Sentimental
Shy	Silly	Smart
Spontaneous	Sympathetic	Tense
Trustworthy	Warm	Wise

CHAPTER FIVE – FREEDOM IN MAKING CHOICES

The importance of knowing that at any moment in time we have the power to make choices is vital to our sense of being in control of our lives. Knowing we can make choices means that we are empowered and not driven by the dictates of what others want us to do and be.

To be in a place where you feel that life has let you down so much, that you don't have anyone to turn to or talk to, that you want to take your own life is a very "brave" and dark place to be. I often wonder what drives someone to the brink of wanting to take their own life and then committing the act. How much emotional pain can someone be in?

Devi Ward was one such person who I interviewed for this book who has been to that place of desperation with thoughts of taking her own life. Yet now she walks tall and proud at making a decision which changed her life around for the better. Here Devi shares powerfully her journey.

"The title of this book is perfectly correct, especially in my case because it was through confronting my deepest "wounding" that I actually found my purpose in life. I do believe that for many of us who are healers, leaders, teachers and educators in these different fields in the healing arts and holistic lifestyle realm, many of us have found our purpose and path. This is because we were in pain and so deeply wounded and it was out of the quest for life, for healing, for transformation that opened us to allow us to become empowered and to become the healers and teachers that we are today. It was through our healing that we became the holders of this knowledge.

For me going through my own "wounded" process there were so many different layers and levels because I have been through so many different transitions which started about twenty years ago. I was in so much pain that I sat down with a bottle of wine, some razors, herbal ecstasies and proceeded to cut my wrists, thinking I was going to commit suicide. It was through that experience for the final time that I confronted my "suicidal tendencies" and decided that suicide was not an option.

With all the screaming, pain and suffering, I couldn't take that final cut, for me, for my friends nor my family. That was my rock bottom but it was the most beautiful thing because it was the thing that catapulted me forward but I had to find a way to live in this world free of pain and that is what I have been doing in the last twenty years. It took me to Hawaii, it took me to the mountains of North Carolina where I became a monk, it took me to the forest in Oregon and eventually bought me to the path of Tibetan Tantra.

So transforming and healing our "wounding" takes courage. We really are confronting our demons which can be terrifying and finding a way to integrate them and understand them as part of our totality, part of our wholeness, part of our individuality and uniqueness and integrating those shadow parts back into our consciousness so that we can become fully integrated, fully functional human beings is a journey in itself. It is not like this journey has been "I know what my wounding is and I'm going to fix it." Most of the time I am blundering around not knowing what my "wounding" is. It was only in the process of healing I realised that I was really wounded.

There is no magic wand to wave and all of a sudden you are going to be fixed. Jung says it is often these shadow parts of ourselves that contain some of the most beautiful, precious, creative, unique gifts we have to offer humanity.

The first thing for me was finding a tool that would effectively get under the pain and uproot it. It's one thing to talk about integrating our pain but how do you do that? So for me the first priority was finding an effective method.

The first thing for me was to reclaim my power by saying "NO". That felt good. I am a physical abuse survivor so being able to say "NO" not to offer any explanation other than to say "NO I don't want to" was huge. So I stopped committing to things I didn't want to commit to, I stopped being out of integrity with my Soul, which is huge. How can we trust ourselves if we keep saying "YES" to things that we don't want to be doing.

Still today there are still layers and layers and I can never say that I am completely done even in the tantric tradition even when you reach enlightenment there are 11 levels of enlightenment so even then you are not done. The ride just goes on and on but it gets better and better.

TOOLS, TIPS AND RECOMMENDATIONS

- Getting support and guidance from someone who has walked the path who can hold you and support you through it, i.e a coach, an educator or a therapist. There is no need to carry stuff on your own.

- A lot of the wounding that we are healing as part of the collective consciousness is part of our culture. So I would encourage you to get support, and feedback, to get a broader view so you take it a lot less personally. Have somebody supporting you through the process of healing because it can get really dark, and you have the support to talk you through the other side.

- To learn to ask for help and have people in your life who you can be totally vulnerable and authentic with where you don't have to put up the facade and mask, someone you can be broken with.

Devi Ward
Founder Certified Authentic Tantra Educator,
Certified Tantric Healer, Author and Radio Host
www.deviwardtantra.com

CHAPTER SIX – HEALING THROUGH SOUND THERAPY – PART I

As part of the many healing modalities which help us deal with our emotions, sound healing is another powerful process. In this chapter you will find out more about how music can help the healing process with an explanation of methods and techniques used.

I spoke to James D'Angelou who runs vocal sound and therapeutic sound courses where he tries to inspire people with his works. Essentially he uses various symbols and ancient meditation techniques to empower people, stating "the healing has nothing to do with me." He says he is not the healer, they have to become the healer. He can only point the way. So here James talks about his practice.

"Everyone who listens to music is practising sound therapy, whether they believe it or not. What is it that is drawing them to a particular type of vibration? That's mysterious but I think it's two fold – it's a resonance factor. Their particular frequencies make up their psychology even the physical body is receptive to the sounds they want to listen to. These musical sounds are altering their frequencies for the better because it's the coming together called sympathetic vibrations. I think there is another factor which is further afield to do with reincarnation that they recognise these sounds, they've heard them before in some shape or form.

The suggestion therefore that when we are in pain we are drawn to a certain resonance or vibration of a particular tune that somehow plays a healing part with our Soul is what's being suggested here. A principle of sound healing is the idea of sympathetic vibration. That you send those vibrations into the space/energy field of the person. Particularly for me it's focussing on the Chakras, the energy centres. Each one represents a psychological part of our nature and as the energy centres hears the sounds, it will be drawn to try to come into synchronisation with those sounds and therefore the spinning wheel will start to move towards its optimum wave. That is the principle upon every so called sound healer's work. It's a kind of self-correcting of the frequencies of the Chakras at all levels. I am not just talking about the physical, but the emotional and I am particularly focussed on the psychological in terms of the Chakras. So for instance you take the solar plexus. The idea is to have your power and use it properly and with authority but you get imbalances. You have people who are simply aggressive which is one extreme where they exhibit in a very aggressive way or where they try to express their authority and come into a space of humility and cowardice, shirking away from things and that is not good either, so both these conditions emotionally could be bought into the centre if we understand the vibrations of that Chakra.

All Chakras hold pain because there are different types of emotions, so if you are in your root Chakra it is about feeling secure. If you are insecure that is going to cause emotional pain. You can go right up through the Chakra centres and each one has its own way of expressing its emotional pain. Different ones have different aspects. But you can't escape the idea that we are calling it pain and therefore individuals may not feel it subtly like that. So a person who is aggressive may not realise that it is emotional pain whereas a person who has cowardice will feel that more in the shyness and will feel that as a kind of pain i.e "I can't, I can't but I know I should." Most certainly the heart is the centre for this idea of emotional pain and that is why we talk about heart-ache, we literally talk about it as pain.

I don't like to use the expression "emotional pain." I more talk about imbalances where you get extremes of character and not the harmony of the centre of it. So a person whose heart Chakra centre is not working becomes very closed, very hard hearted towards people and embittered.

I will use the expression "sound health" when talking about toning and chanting as part of the healing process is singing whatever kind of singing. Singing produces a kind of vibration in terms of the speaking voice and then of course if you sing in harmony with others that adds to the collective.

Yet when I talk about healing I mean wholeness, I'm not talking about a curative thing I mean when the mind, body and spirit are drawn into a unity.

James D'Angelo
Sound Healer and Composer
http://www.soundspirit.co.uk/about.html

HEALING THROUGH SOUND THERAPY – PART II
The BAST Method of Sound Therapy

The British Academy of Sound Therapy (BAST) was the first organisation to formalise sound therapy by offering a qualification with a code of ethics and standards of best practice and was founded in 2000 following 6 years of research and development. Our research and information from the fields of music psychology, ethnomusicology and music therapy have all enriched the ancient knowledge, making it relevant for modern day living.

Sound therapy is the use of a reflective technique as well as a therapeutic sound. We are using specific sounds, combinations of sounds and rhythms which research has shown can alter brainwave frequencies, put people into a very deep state of awareness, increases the haemoglobin A in the bloodstream (which stimulates the immune system) and reduces stress, which in turn may decrease the amount of cortisol (stress hormone) in the system.

The BAST method uses specific instruments, tools and techniques to affect the physical and psychological levels. After a treatment we ask the client to reflect on their experience during the treatment. We then use a series of questions which we call 'reflective enquiry' with the aim of healing the person to gain valuable insight into their life and symptoms. So for example, if someone came feeling anxious I would ask them about what it was that made them feel anxious. This identifies what is impeding flow, or holding them back. I would ask them to identify where that was in the body and to tell me more about how their anxiety manifests and impacts their life. I would then work with a reflective framework known as the '5Rs: The Cooper Sax Model of Experiential Processing' – we call it the 5Rs for short!

The 5Rs are - Resonance, Resistance, Release, Reflection and Responsibility. They are keys to personal transformation. They are the only five things anyone needs to live a blissful stress-free life!

Activity

For a moment close your eyes and think about a time in your life when you felt absolutely incredible and inhabit that feeling in the body. Try not to attach to the story of it, just feel the feelings.

Now breathing in feel it in your body and magnify it by 10. Notice how that feels. Once you've breathed that feeling into every pore of your being now imagine something you've read in a newspaper or on TV that wasn't so good, something that upset you. Feel that in the body. Notice how your body and energy feels and now bring the feelings from the first visualisation back, breathing it in and filling you up, melting the second feeling away. Reflect on how you felt with the first visualisation – people usually use words such as 'light, bright, open, expanded, joyful' to explain how they felt.

To describe the second visualisation people use words like 'dark, contracted, anxious, fearful and painful'. The first visualisation created a resonance in the system which was experienced as expansion. This is a natural state that we could all experience if we were resonating with our life as love. The second visualisation created Resistance so the beliefs you had around those things that you didn't enjoy seeing impeded that blissful flow resulting in feeling dark, contracted and anxious.

So that is first-hand experience of how energy follows thought (known as the observer effect in quantum physics). Our energy follows our intentions, so you cast your mind to that wonderful thing and your energy expanded, you cast your mind to that not so wonderful thing and your energy contracted.

The next 'R' is Release which can be experienced as tears, laughter or the release of tension in the body - however it manifests to us. Release shows us that there was resistance present. The next part of the process is Reflection. When we really tune into ourselves and reflect on what we are telling ourselves we are able to transform our health and wellbeing. The final state of the process is Responsibility; each and every person is responsible for their process. You know yourself more than anyone else knows you – you are the only one in your head. When you fully embrace that you are the only one responsible for how you feel then you are firmly in the driving seat of your own process. This is a big one for some people to grasp as it seems very easy to blame others, but the reality is that we can only make ourselves feel, think, say and do things – we always have a choice.

At BAST we work in a very non-directive client centred way so the client is the person who knows themselves best. Once the client has talked about their process and what they would like to work on (this can be mental, physical or emotional dis-ease) we then create a 'sonic prescription' to suit the client's individual needs. The intention of a BAST Method sound therapy treatment is to enable the system to remember that lovely wave (resonance) feeling that we would have if we looked at life through the lens of love rather than fear. This is achieved by using certain instruments and playing techniques that enable the client to achieve an elevated state of consciousness during which time there may be some kind of conversation that sound is having with their system. They may all of a sudden have an insight into how they can go about releasing that 'thing' that impedes flow in their life or the resistance may just melt into insignificance - they may think 'why am I holding onto this?'

So in a nutshell the BAST Method of Sound Therapy is the process of carefully designed therapeutic sound, plus the reflective techniques to take the client on a transformational journey within.

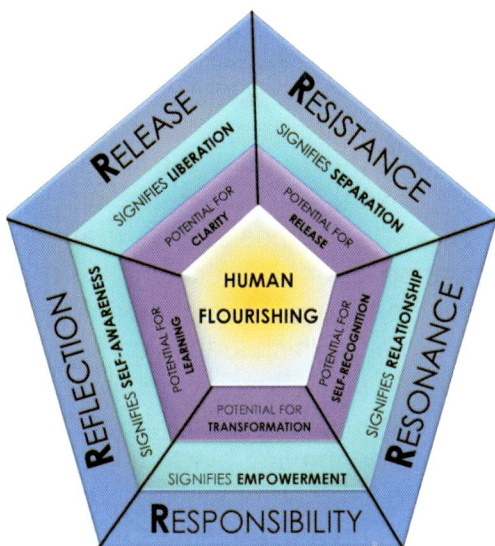

Lyz Cooper
Therapeutic Sound Healer
www.healthysound.com

CHAPTER SEVEN – STANDING TALL WHILST FEELING SMALL

Many of us we have grown up with experiences of racism, prejudice, being bullied, ostracised, feeling different for whatever reason. Often times these experiences and memories influence and can effect who we are, how we perceive the world, our role in the world which then becomes our truth and which lodges as some sort of emotional hurt and pain. Grace Ononiwu shares how she used her pain and rejection to ride on the shoulders of success to become the first black woman to be made Chief Prosecutor in Northamptonshire. Here Grace shares her journey and the amazing experiences which influenced and moulded her into the very successful person she is today.

"I remember making the decision when I was 8 that I wanted to be a Lawyer because my dad had been stopped for speeding and I remember saying to him "don't worry daddy when I get older I will represent you." I'm not sure I really knew what it meant by the word "represent" but I knew in my young mind it was standing up and representing my dad and then of course everything I've done has been focussed on that activity. I used to enjoy watching Crown Court. I was intrigued by the wigs and the gowns and I thought I'd really like to do that.

My parents always told me I could be anything I put my mind to. For them it was important that I was a good child. I had to listen to what my teachers told me as they knew better and if I followed their guidance I wouldn't go wrong. It wasn't until I was 14 when I went along to the local recruitment fair at school that I felt my dreams had been shattered. I remember having a conversation with my teacher, telling her my dreams. It was the first time I had voiced what I had wanted to do when I grew up. I told her I wanted to be a Lawyer and her instant reaction was I couldn't do that and she gave me a hundred reasons why and not one reason why I could. I remembered what my mother and father had told me about listening to teachers and I thought what's the point? I felt so disappointed and I think it was my first real memory of feeling that weight of disappointment. This is not to say I always got what I wanted up until that point but it did hit me quite significantly. It affected my behaviour and my attitude. I didn't work hard anymore and I messed around with friends and then I failed all my exams. I remember going home to explain this to my mother. The weight of disappointment on her face and her telling me "so that's what you are worth" had a huge impact on me. I didn't like how failure made me feel because it caused me a great deal of embarrassment and that failure was something I wasn't prepared to endure again. So I used that as an anchor to go and re-visit my exams which I passed.

I then went on to Hatfield Polytechnic where I did my Degree and met with people from different walks of life. It was a fun environment, but when I left and went to The Guildford College of Law to do my professional exam to become a solicitor that's when I realised how out of sorts I was. I shouldn't be where I am today because on paper I didn't go to the right schools or University. I didn't come from the right background. The legal profession is one of the oldest professions in this country so it's incredibly traditionalist and it wasn't where someone like me should be. Everybody was connected. Very few people looked like me. Either daddy or uncle owned a firm, or daddy's friend owned a firm or daddy was head of chambers and they had connections, many of them had their articles sorted out. It was almost as if I was apologising for my presence, that I didn't have a right to be there and I had the added challenge with my colleagues because not only did I have to try to pass exams I also had to manage my insecurities, yet I got through them. I remember sending 70 letters out to various firms for work experience and I got one response back because when you see my name, Grace Ononiwu, you know who I am and it was obvious that was the position and that hurt. Then one chance came along and I thought to myself I am going to go for it because if they meet me I will get a chance and I was right because they offered me the job and it was then my journey began.

When I left there and joined the Crown Prosecution Service I did every legal job in the CPS until the historical appointment in 2005 when I was appointed Chief Prosecutor in North Hamptonshire which made me the first person of African Heritage to hold that post and I was the first black person and woman to hold the post as well. I remember thinking that I could focus on the disappointments and expecting to be disappointed. I could focus on how hurtful it was to be judged without people knowing you and assumptions being made about my abilities but it's not worth allowing that to influence how I behave and felt about myself because I realised that in doing this I was not giving myself a chance. I've realised that most people spend their time on the things that they do not do well. So I focussed on my strengths. I am aware of the things that I do not do well. This journey has helped me have greater clarity of purpose which has given me greater confidence because what I am really clear about is that I focus on the things I know as I know me and I want to give myself a chance.

"That doesn't mean I don't respect pain nor respect what has happened because it is important to acknowledge that but actually in acknowledging it the question therefore is what steps are you then taking to move forward and that is what I have done over the years."

TOOLS, TIPS AND RECOMMENDATIONS

- Once you make the decision to put down your pain give yourself permission to put it down. That doesn't mean that you don't respect pain or that you are under-estimating the significance of what has happened to you but you can't change what's happened. What you can do is YOU and not to let what's happened define your future in a negative way.

- Trying to deal with the pain look at how you can move forward. For some people it takes time. You've got to give yourself permission to take that time. I keep talking about giving yourself permission. People tend to be harder on themselves than anyone else. The advice I would give is to ensure that negativity (and I think pain is a negativity, it's not a good feeling, it hurts and anything that hurts is not good) does not define who you are.

- What you can achieve in the future doesn't define how you engage with others. It really is important that people have the confidence and give themselves permission to deal with their issues and unpack them and deal with them. People have different experiences some may be small, some may be quite significant and the amount of time it takes to work through these depends on the circumstances. Yet one thing that is sure is that we do not allow ourselves to become a victim but actually start thinking about being a survivor.

Grace Ononiwu, OBE
Chief Crown Prosecutor for the West Midlands, UK

CHAPTER EIGHT – REMAINING AUTHENTIC WHILST STANDING ON THE SHOULDERS OF PAIN

Internationally acclaimed author Patricia Cori is one of the most well-known and established authorities on the realms of the mystic views of the world that challenge the status quo. With thirteen books, published in more than twenty foreign languages, she has been a key voice in the alternative media for decades, bringing paradigm-busting information to the public since 1996.

I wanted to capture Patricia Cori's experience because I felt she stood for honesty, authenticity and openness which can be rare in a world where many who are in the public eye have the courage to be themselves, to share their pain openly and to stand authentically in their truth. Patricia is not afraid to say "I feel exposed, vulnerable, I hurt, I cry, I feel pain." In that place it makes it easier for us to look at our shadow side, those aspects of ourselves which we often sweep under the carpet. I hope that through Patricia sharing her story and journey that somehow her insight will resonate with you in some way.

"It's fascinating at this time of incredible difficulty on earth that a lot of spiritual teachers, healers and people in positions to help others find their way through the very intense polarity we are going through, are also being tested and tested to the max. I consider myself a spiritual warrior. I am out there fighting for the whales, trying to make a difference, helping people as much as possible to get a grasp on both sides of this shift both the dark and the light. I find that I too am going through some incredible tests. I think it's a time when the wheat is being separated from the shaft in terms of who people really are, who claim they are spiritual and how they walk their talk.

I am going through a rather big challenge at this moment as I've just broken up with my partner and Soul-mate of 29 years. I believe that Soul-mates come together and separate. Sometimes it's not always happy land and over the rainbow when you re-unite with a Soul-mate. Despite all of that, the more I am stripped of things that I understood as security, comfort and safety (although I am not a person who lives in "safe" very much) and the more these challenges come in, the stronger I feel spiritually. That makes me so excited because I am being tested, my spirit is being tested and I am standing tall in my truth. Despite the emotional upheaval I feel my purpose even more, I feel clarity and I feel determined.

Experiencing any sort of emotional pain as you go through this process feels and looks like there is a huge hollow in my heart because when you've been with someone and loved someone that long and suddenly there's a break up, at the beginning there is a sort of shock and then you go through a process. It starts off in the root Chakra, it cuts your sense of survival, you don't know where you are, you loose your ground as if someone has pulled the carpet from under your feet. Then you move up into the emotional body, where you are all over the place.

"We must remember that we came into this life to have a range of emotions, from pain to joy and I really believe that being a healer for so many years the last thing you want to do is to block pain. It causes cancer or worse in the body, so I am going to release that pain and that is a very difficult process because this means there is lots of crying, doubt and deep sorrow."

Then it moves into the Power Chakra where it's about any anger that is attached to it and a sense of powerlessness and rising above that in order to be able to bring it into the Heart Chakra and then to let it go and forgive it.

Because I've been a healer for so many years it has been easier for me to move on. Some people may feel a month is a short time but I know how energy moves and how it gets blocked. In a relationship you don't recognise that it's deteriorating because it becomes a very comfortable habit. With my partner I've been in this very comfortable habit not realising that there were things that were missing and if they were missing for me they were missing for him too.

I believe that you can't move on until you reach that place of acceptance. There is a point where two people can say this isn't working anymore. Whatever the thing is that you know is causing you pain it's your job to pull that cord out, detach from the co-dependency, cut the umbilical cord with the other person and let it go.

I am meditating every morning and doing everything possible to stay in balance. I've gotten rid of emotional triggers which are dangerous. Anything that triggers emotion about the relationship – pictures, jewellery, everything is gone. I am practising right mind and when my mind starts going back to the wound I just say "Nope you can't go there." Bearing in mind I had my days of extreme pain, crying and hysterics so a lot of it I really processed it out. I eliminated the emotional triggers and turned my attention to "what do I need to do to completely free myself from this situation?"

I am a very heart centred person and had been hiding out a bit so that the worst of the emotions could be dealt with. When this happened I had two days of hysterics. I got on a plane and flew to Glastonbury where I was nurtured by some incredibly supportive and very spiritual people who helped me stay on track. One in particular said "you know this is for your highest good don't you? You must have known on some level that this was coming?" and I did. I rarely ask people for help and it was wonderful to say "I'm in trouble" and people rallied for me and that was another reason why I am so much better so quickly.

The true healer needs to be a lighthouse for people who come to him or her. You might have a great technique but if you are to be considered a true spirit, warrior or healer you've got to walk the talk. I feel at this moment in time, I'm being given the opportunity to really test my metal. My partner is helping because he is not acting very well but if he was acting better it would probably be more emotional for me, so this is helping me get stronger. One thing I think that is my essence is that I walk my talk. It's been tested over and over again and I have to thank my mother a lot for that because she was a person who walked her talk a lot.

TOOLS TIPS AND RECOMMENDATIONS

- The first thing is to try to detach emotionally and ask yourself a series of questions I.e "What am I loosing here?" Make a list. I am a firm believer in the T-Bar process which is where you create a list using Pros and Cons. So you ask yourself a series of questions and then note down their pros and cons giving them a score from 1-10. So you can ask yourselves questions like How happy was I? How did the relationship make me feel? Did we communicate well?

- Don't look for people to commiserate with. We tend to vilify the person in question with our friends. Then we keep going over the situation time and time again which means we give away our power in order to heal ourselves. If you are looking for help where people can have a perspective on where you are coming from and where you are going in order to help you heal that is ok, but if they are serving as a sounding board then all you are doing is turning your power over to the story and prolonging the time it will take to heal.

- You've got to really stand up and look at yourself and say I'm not a baby any more. I'm a big girl or boy now. I've got to do this. It's hard and hopefully you can find a friend or parent or someone who really loves you. I think as far as clinical steps that need to be taken, you need to get away from the situation. Distance is key to be with people who really care and love you. Then you get distance between yourself and the pain. But getting away from all the triggers is important.

- Remorse - If someone starts to have remorse it can be a trigger - "Are you ok?, I miss you."

- It's hard - but that's life. We came here to have a human experience and it is one of an immense range of emotions. What I celebrate about emotions and pain is that it makes you stronger. It makes you better and then you can work on getting over "it." It's part of finality so you can move on and then you can reach new heights.

Patricia Cori
World Renowned Author, Teacher, Lecturer and
Spiritual Guide to ancient spiritual sites
http://www.patriciacori.com

CHAPTER NINE – HOW EMOTIONAL DEFICITS CREATES DYSFUNCTION

For some reason this year I've been drawn to horses, to understand how they facilitate very profound and in-depth healing of the human emotion. Another "How to" process using the horse as a facilitator to reach and dissolve pain as horses are highly spiritual beings who mirror our truth and reflect exactly how we are feeling. I was also interested and drawn to healing horses who had physical and emotional pain and wounds and I loved the experience because of what it did for me as well. An exchange of energy and healing took place which was a very profound experience.

The working on healing horses came about because I had the privilege of giving someone an Intuitive Reading over the phone in 2014. She then asked me to tell her what was going on with her horse and I was able to describe his emotions and also describe and see in thermal imagery any pain he was carrying on a physical and emotional level. I was then invited to visit the horse a few weeks later and conducted a hands on healing on him to great success. A week later the owner contacted me to say that the horse was much more receptive to being ridden, and that some of the pain I had picked up had gone.

I then decided to investigate more about the healing power of horses and came across an internet article by Cindy Jarrett, a Communications and Relationship Consultant, Shamanic Practitioner and Equine Experiential Learning Facilitator. What struck me most about this article was not so much what Cindy said about horses, but more so about the state of humanity's consciousness around their own emotions and inner truth. The fear to be authentic, honest and truthful, the fear to lay down pain and the ability to speak our truth is such a huge part of whether we stay stuck emotionally or heal past pain. Here is an article Cindy wrote which I felt compelled to use in my book, primarily because of its very strong sentiments and importance.

"Horses are sentient and highly intuitive, social animals who sense fear, uncertainty and emotional distress. In EFEL workshops, horses act as facilitators for participants who are discovering underlying problems. By acting as a mirror, clients can identify problems they are experiencing that enables them to make relevant changes towards a more peaceful and fulfilled life where they can work on building confidence, self-esteem, learn to trust and have patience, enhance communication and listening skills and strengthen relationships by improving emotional understanding and discipline.

Horses open your heart and when you look and listen through the lens of your heart, you open the doorway to the language and world of feeling. In this land of feeling comes all our emotions, our intuition, our bodily sensations, our sensory information, and our soul's voice each uniquely rich with their own valuable wisdom.

How life works for horses in a herd is by knowing the consciousness of each member within the herd and their environment in order to survive. Where is the lead mare standing? Where is the water and food? Where is the safe ground? What are the weather patterns? Knowing where there might be a predator lurking. Who are their friends? What is the order of leadership? Is it time for play or rest?

This cannot be effectively managed within the herd if its members are disconnected from their feelings/ sensory awareness or disconnected with each other and surroundings. They prefer to depend on each other.

We humans have been taught by example and verbal direction to not be open with most of our emotions. This has caused a cultural crisis in being cut off emotionally for hundreds of years. This has had a cumulative effect of a lot of unexpressed and repressed emotions. We sit on a cultural emotional volcano with more and more people expressing their unfounded judgments, rage and hostility at a moment's notice.

In the human community we rarely grow-up in an environment of knowing what other family members are really thinking or feeling. Much of this is assumed, hidden, or denied. There is a lot of guessing, making things up, projecting, and judging that comes from the fallout of poor relationships with our emotional nature. We learn it is wrong to ask questions. We often don't get the opportunity to practice effective relationship and communication skills."

I found the above piece incredibly powerful since it has been something I have been working on in my own life. I am learning more and more the importance of operating from a place of being open and authentic as much as I can. This has often been met with resistance by many simply because of the fear it takes to be totally honest and truthful. I then felt compelled to contact Cindy to interview her especially to further elaborate on the subject of humanity's lack of emotional intelligence because it is such an important and huge subject. Here Cindy she shares her viewpoint.

"We have family systems that are predominantly driven by dealing with the emotional content from each member in that system in reactive ways. This reactivity is never our highest truth. We often don't remember what we are saying and we certainly are not very aware of its impact. This reactivity is often driven from the bankrupted systems of aggressive, passive or passive aggressive communication models and a whole lot of unfinished emotional content. Listening is often lost which is one of the most important components to effective communication when dealing with emotional content.

Within high reactive relating we just do not hear each other well. We rarely get to solutions from a reactive place. Wants and needs get lost in non-listening and then solutions cannot be properly accessed either. The fall out ends up creating a lot of recycling, unheard content. This dynamic is what I call our *'Emotional Spin-Cycle Self'*. It tends to be a recycling dynamic in how people express their emotions, often rife with complaining, which means they are registering the complaint but rarely reaching honest solutions. So by getting in touch with what you want and need and then taking right action to discover appropriate solutions you stay connected to what I also call your *'Emotionally Creative Self'*. The Emotional Spin Cycle Self or ESCS needs to act as merely a hailing devise to get your attention that something is wanting and needing your attention not a place to be relating from, that's the good news about the ESCS.

The ESCS is loaded with information that lets us know we are out of balance, that we need help. Something needs our attention but what happens people tend to work or talk from that reactive place instead of use it as information, a hailing device to wake-up to something. So we don't want to get rid of this mechanism because they are like receptors in our hands which tell us to move our hands off a hot burner that we didn't know was on. We need something that tells us we are out of balance and to use it merely as a hailing device vs. live our lives from there. This just isn't our highest truth. Reactivity distorts and we are being our lesser self not our higher self in those moments.

The reason therefore, why we don't tell the truth is because everyone who has told the truth when growing up has usually been punished. So consequently if we are being authentic, which is expressing the truth, this can appear as a threatening act to a lot of people who are lost in immaturity, because they don't have the ego strength or ability to deal with it. How we get to truthful relating is by dealing with it in stages, because you can't just start blurting out all your truth in certain relationships ill- equipped for that content.

How we deal with truth with family members was another segment of our discussion. "Well, you can't just start telling the truth because you are ready to tell the truth now. You have to go back to foundational work when you are bringing truth into a system that has never had it nor ever experienced it in its authentic expression.

One needs to make sure their commitments are aligned and ensure that all persons involved are committed to telling the truth to each other without causing harm. Once you establish aligned commitment then you have to establish some operating agreements, like agreeing to not hold onto anything. Or, when we tell the truth we do it with love, kindness and care. That we check things out for meaning and intention vs assuming or projecting onto the other person. We use the tool and practice of active listening and active mirroring. We agree to not get defensive, and to bring wisdom. When we are dealing with our diversity which fuels all conflict, we are dealing with having to tell the truth. This is why it is so important to establish new ground rules and agreements before jumping into the deep end when there has been no pattern of workability in the past. Working out deep feelings and conflict requires structure and emotional discipline.

You cannot overstep these two foundational pieces of committing to being aligned and making agreements when you begin to express truth newly. This is true for work environments, as well as Beloved or friendship relationships.

Something to bear in mind is that some people are ahead of themselves with their intention to tell the truth but lack the ability to do so. So when people are promising ability that may or may not be present, you have to look and see whether they are trustworthy, can they deliver? It takes a lot of tending and conversations around the crafting of the agreements and starting small instead of "let's talk about the affair we had" to "let's talk about how we do the dishes and do the laundry differently that causes us to argue, etc." You have to work up to the heart of the issues of hurtful content in most unfinished emotional business in a family system."

TIPS, TOOLS AND RECOMMENDATIONS

- The Truth shall set you free. Standing in your truth, is a value and a value that is backed by practice. You can have a high value but if it's not backed by practice then you are incongruent and you are not in a truthful relationship with self and soul.

- To really have and be an authentic person you will need to stand for truth. It needs to be a value of yours. You will need to bring a vow of non-harming and non--attachment because in order to live authentically, people who know you well can and will feel threatened. There is great responsibility to be taken when opening up old or new relationships to more truthful relating.

- Because we're not geared towards this honest revealing of our feeling states, this is where horse medicine comes in because horses thrive in knowing the truthful feeling state of every herd member for survival. They can model for us this safe space of non-judgment when expressing truthful emotions. People being in the presence of horses in a workshop environment begin to decipher their true self, their true voice, because horses respond quickly to truth and non-truth.

Cindy Jarrett is a Communications and Relationship Consultant, owner of Designing Access for the past 25 years; Cindy is also a Shamanic Practitioner for 22 years.
http://www.horsejourneys.com/emotional.html

CHAPTER TEN – EFFECTIVE COMMUNICATION WITH SELF, EFFECTIVE COMMUNICATION WITH OTHERS

How someone recognises they need healing or are carrying wounds all comes down to happiness. This should be the gauge to which we perceive our life experiences. If a person wants to realise whether they have baggage, trauma baggage, pain or hurt baggage one of the things to ask is Am I Happy? How long have I not been happy? What percentage of my life have I been happy? and What percentage have I not been happy?

The unhappiness that we experience in life is a clear indicator that we have some healing to do. You will find that those who suffer the most and experience high levels of trauma in their childhood experience high levels of unhappiness in adulthood therefore if you want to get to the core issues of trauma, hurt or pain then look at your own happiness which is the great gauge.

So if I look at my childhood and most of my early adulthood, I realise I was unhappy then I realised I had my own things I needed to deal with. Once I decided to deal with that healing process which was often difficult and also challenging the more I healed and the more happiness I began to experience. If a person wants to get an idea of whether or not they need to engage in their own healing process then look at the happiness factor in their lives and use this as a barometer to measure whether healing needs to take place.

That happiness factor is not adversely impacted so easily. It's not something external of you that makes you happy it's a state of mind. You may see things on the periphery on the external that gives you the illusion that you are happy i.e someone gives you something, you buy a car or piece of jewellery but that is all externally driven and influenced so easily by the external.

I can use my own relationship with myself and my wife. Before we got together we were working on our own self healing but when we got together we established enough personal healing where we were operating collectively and now we have had 13 years of healing together. But we also had to engage and prepare for that interaction. For those of us who have engaged in the healing process and are actively committed to the healing process and are more in line with realising happiness in our lives it is that experience of what people call love which is more in line with the truth of what love is.

Who makes a comment like this? is it the person who is truly happy or the person who perceives they are happy? "Love hurts." It is only the person who is hurt, who is unhappy, the person who has been traumatised, who associates love with hurt. For people who have not developed a level of happiness in their lives, they may be under an illusion of their pain so they accept pain, suffering and hurt in place of love, because their unhappiness jades their vision of what love is. This is one of the great issues people face in terms of relationships. It's perceived through the lens of hurt. So therefore love hurts.

Conversely someone like my wife and I know this because we've experienced true love. The person who experiences true love knows that love does not hurt. That's the great thing about coming into a relationship where you engage in that relationship and now you can heal together which elevates the happiness factor therefore the level of love in that relationship is seen through the lens of happiness and now you can say that love heals.

Now about alignment. For me it's about two people working towards a collective goal that manifests and materialises high levels of love. That is what all this healing process is about. Most people think the healing process is getting rid of stuff, the baggage, the things that are holding us back that is part of it but ultimately the healing process is about clearing out the space, healing thyself ,clearing out the negativity, getting into a state of mind of abundance, abundance consciousness because love is abundance. In other words the healing process is the opening goal to materialise happiness so we can experience higher levels of love. That is what happened to myself and my wife only because we came into alignment and only because prior to coming together we had engaged in a level of healing that prepared us for that alignment and as we built upon it we experienced a higher level of love.

TIPS, TOOLS AND RECOMMENDATIONS

- There is always an internal process going on with the healing process. With you asking questions like What am I feeling now? Why am I feeling this way? Where does this feeling come from? This is where we have to speak to ourselves and as you do that the answers come.

- Making a strong commitment to your healing process the answers come from within. We should be kind and loving enough to have those internal conversations with ourselves.

- Also communication is the most important thing in relationships.   Communication is so valuable that we should definitely have high levels of communication as part of our healing process especially when it comes to our heart. When we engage with someone else who is engaged or assisting us in a healing process or they are actively engaged in their own healing process and we are journeying together in alignment that communication is so very important.

Lenon Honor
Husband, Father, Author, Counsellor, Musician
www.lenonhonor.com

CHAPTER ELEVEN – DANCING INTO YOUR EMOTIONS: RELEASING THROUGH MOVEMENT

"One of the joys of my life is dancing. It's a wonderful cathartic play with movement and joy and release. Whenever I have needed to fully express myself in order to release stress or just to take myself out of my situation into a place that captures me and holds me and embraces my pain, I either listen to music, I exercise or I dance and in that place everything seems to fade away."

Wyoma

I had the greatest of pleasures in interviewing a highly intuitive woman with a passion for movement. Movement to me is another form of expression which heals, transforms, shifts and transcends. I had seen Wyoma's videos a few years previously, so it was a wonderful surprise when I emailed this lady and she graciously accepted my request to be interviewed. In the below interview Wyoma really holds and nurtures a space for us to enter into as she talks about the wisdom of ancient knowledge through dance and movement.

Esther: Who is Wyoma in a nutshell?

Wyoma: I am a holistic health healer, dancer and interested in civilisation, transformation and any way possible and any means necessary I love movement.

Esther: How can movement help us with our healing? On a general basis.

Wyoma: There are so many aspects to movement which is a part of the tradition of the human experience. We are given these bodies because we are supposed to move and so if you connect your physical movement with your spiritual, mental and emotional it's always much more powerful when everything is working together. You connect the thoughts that you are having to your movement and part of it helps to move the cells along. It's part of the alignment actually moving energy, so to move energy you have to move your body. Movement changes your brain when you move. That was one of my earliest recognitions in my 20's when I was contemplating a career. I experienced how different I felt after I had gone out dancing or after I had taught a class or performed. My energy always shifted and whatever was bugging me before wasn't bugging me after. That was my first recognition. Movement was essential for change.

Esther: Are you able to elaborate how movement helps the brain?

Wyoma: Movement helps the brain because certain brain chemicals are released i.e serotonin, dopamine, oxytocin. When you start to move it connects us to ancient memories and ancient wisdom in our bodies and we have more access to that part that is in our brains as it allows us a kind of release. Esther, I like it when you mentioned about your experience of dancing where you said it felt as if you had fireflies under your feet. That is beautiful and the kind of release I am talking about. Yet what is unique is that there is a lot of memory insight and wisdom into who we are as spiritual human beings and this movement ritual connection connects us to ancient wisdom and movement and the knowledge that goes with it. So there is a lot that happens when we access that part of our brains which holds that wisdom.

Esther: I like how you always connect things back to our spirituality and ancient wisdom. I would surmise that for a lot of people dance is an expression but I don't feel they really understand the real level of consciousness that dance takes you into. The enriched depth of self and understanding self, empowering us to release aspects of who we are. So what does it mean to be able to tap into that ancient space within us? What is that ancient space?

Wyoma: One of the aspects that I do in African Healing Dance is the practice of one-ness. It is a belief that we are all connected that we are all one and we are all on our individuated journey on our way back to our soul source and there are many paths of doing that but we are all connected. I started practising yoga when I was 18 so part of the philosophy is that everything is happening at once which means we are omnipresent, omnipotent, omniscient. Everything is happening at once and I think the more opened up we are and the more clear we are we have more access to WHO we are. Our body movement assists with that. We are more in touch with all of ourselves, our ancient selves, our current self, our male self, our female self, our child self, our adult self, all aspects of who we are.

Though we get isolated, separated and put in boxes as to who we are and what's possible about what we can do, when we move and when we get more deeply connected with ourselves that whole space becomes timeless and unlimited. You really connect with deep aspects of yourself and it feels more like an archetypal knowing that's beyond and that's the feeling that comes up when I move and what comes up when I'm sitting in meditation and any kind of meditation experience as well as working with people.

So Esther in response to the statement that through movement, there seems to be an essence of creating rituals and manifesting through the movements I do, most definitely because when I dance, the way I use my hands that's an expression. The way I hold my body is an expression so through that process we are using and creating rituals as part of that process of movement.

There are some African traditional movements for instance which is planting and harvesting or bringing into your heart, sharing love into the heart out from the heart and moving energy up from the air, honouring the elements.

Movement allows you to express your emotions whatever they are. Many people say they dance to sadness but I've never been able to stay sad when I am dancing. I'm enjoying the sadness, I'm accepting that state, there is something more rounded about it if I'm moving.

Wyoma
Dance Performance Artist and Teacher, USA
www.wyomadance.com

CHAPTER TWELVE – FACING DENIAL AND DEALING WITH TRUTH

If you are going through an emotional break up on many levels how do you keep things together? How do you keep an emotional balance when you feel you are being dissected, pulled apart and every area of your life seems to be falling apart? Where do you go to exhale? How do you keep a handle on things? Here Gayle Edwards shares one of those moments in her life when things came to a standstill and the emotional struggle and impact this had on her own self-esteem and identify.

"It all started when I separated from my husband, my dad became ill, subsequently died and I had a car accident during the same time. Each one of those experiences would've been enough on their own but put them all together and I started to feel very unworthy, very lonely. My dad was my world and when he was no longer there I felt I had no-where to go and I became numb for quite a long time. Not having my husband at the time to turn to because of our situation left me feeling very isolated because my mum was going through her own stuff as well and even though I am an only child, lots of people would say you've got to be strong for your mum. So I was fulfilling that role and I didn't feel at that time that there was anyone fulfilling that role for me and it took me a year before I could even grieve.

How that grieving process did eventually start was a very good friend came around to see me and said that every time she had seen me for the past 6 months I'd been wearing the same thing and she asked me what was going on. I remember disagreeing with her being in complete denial. Then she said "ok take off those jeans" and she threw them through the window. I looked at them and instead of feeling embarrassed I suddenly felt released and relieved because somebody had noticed me and that is what started the process of me getting myself back together and starting to explore different techniques and resources that were going to help me to help myself as well.

Emotionally what happened was like the key that unlocked the door because I couldn't be strong then, I couldn't hold it all in my stiff upper lip my way. I had to let it go. The door had been opened and there was no turning back. A real rush of emotions came through and also what came through at the time was a feeling of selfishness. I had this urge to get myself sorted. My daughter was only three at the time and in the process of all of this my husband and I had reconciled, which in hindsight probably was not the best time to be reconciling because my emotions were all over the place, but it was at that time I felt I needed to put myself first.

The one thing that helped me more than anything else was the Emotional Freedom Technique (EFT) because you are not only able to start working on yourself in a short space of time, but you are able to release so much in a very accelerated amount of time.

Ancient times have taught us that because of our meridian lines we are all energy so anything that we can do to tap into those meridian lines and change things and remove those blocks you have to experience it for yourself.

Neuro Linguistic Programming (NLP) was another great tool which helped me tremendously. It is how we interpret what is going on in our brains and the actions we are taking and the language we use. I remember walking into the training course dressed a bit like the Grim Reaper wearing all black. I was dressed how I felt that day and sat at the back of the class. I thought if I just sit here with my notebook we'd get this done quickly and I will get my certificate at the end of the week. I remember the trainer pointing at me asking me to sit at the front and I thought "I can't do this, I don't want to sit at the front" so I said "Im ok here." Then he said "why are you here?" and I said because I want to help more of my clients and he said "well I can tell you now, that is not what we do here so it's your choice. You can either sit at the front and participate in what we do or you can leave because it's the wrong course for you." So I thought, OK, so I said "what do you do here?" and he said do you want to come and sit at the front so that we can get started and I can tell you? So I reluctantly went to the front and sat down vex, of course, because I'm thinking this guy has now challenged me. It soon became very clear that I was going to be my first client. He explained that "what we do here is not help you to help other people but help you to help yourself" and that was definitely the most life changing week of my life. NLP is now part of my whole life and my whole being that I don't even realise I am doing it the whole time.

TIPS, TOOLS AND RECOMMENDATIONS

- Find something that works for you. I found that NLP and EFT were extremely powerful, practical and instant tools that I could use in my everyday life.

- Find someone who knows you and who you can be accountable to.

- Being honest with yourself is sometimes the hardest thing to be, but as the saying goes "The Truth will set you free."

Gayle Edwards
The Breakthru Diva
www.breakthrudiva.com

CHAPTER THIRTEEN – SPEAKING OUT MY PAIN INTO WHOLENESS

I had a very scarred childhood from the age of 4 up until the age of 16. I've experienced lots of traumatic events and didn't get any professional help as my mum said we should leave it to God, bless her but these experiences crept up over the years. Life has been a roller-coaster but I think it's made me stronger for who I am today and I ask myself would I be here if these things didn't happen?

How I've have kept sane over the last five to ten years has been through public speaking and from people saying to me "I've been through something similar thank you for sharing because I've not shared anything or spoken to anyone about what happened to me". The sanity part has come from speaking out and sharing and that has helped me to heal.

One of my many traumatic experiences was when I was about 10 and my hair caught on fire. My hair was in Gerry Curl and was very long and bouncy. My mother had gone to college and my little brother was sleeping. I was waiting for my stepfather to come home which was literally about a 30 minute wait. I decided I was hungry and when I tried to light the cooker my hair caught fire. I knocked on my neighbours door and when no-one answered in order to get the heat out I put hot water on my head which made things worst. I found that incident extremely hard to deal with but the hardest part was when woke up the next day in hospital and looked in the mirror and saw what happened. That was painful because I had blisters coming down my face and no hair and suffered second degree burns. I have two scars on my head where the hair will never grow back because the burns were so severe.

One of my other life defining moments which I found the most difficult was the fact that my mother came to London at the age of 20 into an arranged marriage. The man she came to marry was 15 years older and he beat the living daylights out of her. She suffered so much domestic violence to the extent when you look at her arm she still has a big cigarette stamp there and when I look at that it makes me feel really sad.

I've never had counselling in my whole life until 2013 when a colleague of mine died and someone suggested I go for bereavement counselling. Even though we were talking about bereavement, the sessions bought up a lot of other things from my past. It was these sessions that helped me to heal.

TIPS, TOOLS AND RECOMMENDATIONS

- Seek professional help and talk to and hang around the right people. There are people who act like they are there for you but they are not. They are very hard to identify, so you need to make sure you find a trusted source.

- If you are good at writing, write things down, if you like speaking speak.

- One thing I did for a long time was to beat myself up about things that had happened. Then I asked myself "why should I beat myself up about something I have no control over?" Whether it was my fault or not, whether it was meant to be or not I realise I needed to be able to understand that I don't have control over what happens at times and I couldn't blame myself for this and I needed to basically get up and move on.

- One thing about pain and the past is it can hold you back, because you can remain in a time warp. The way I see life now is that whatever happened happened. I can't erase that from my mind but the good thing is that I am still alive. Life is about trying to be positive which can be difficult at times but it's a process and it takes time because you can't rush these things.

Mavis Amankwah
Multi-Award Winning Entrepreneur,
PR Guru, Author, Motivational Speaker,
Business Coach, Wealth Creator
http://mavisamankwah.com

CHAPTER FOURTEEN – THE POWER OF LAUGHTER

Laughter Yoga – A complete exercise for Body Mind and Spirit

What is Laughter Yoga? Laughter Yoga combines unconditional laughter with yogic breathing (PRANAYAMA). Anyone can laugh for no reason, without relying on humour, jokes or comedy. Laughter is simulated as a body exercise in a group but with eye contact and childlike playfulness, it soon turns into real and contagious laughter. The concept of Laughter Yoga is based on a scientific fact that the body cannot differentiate between fake and real laughter. One gets the same physiological and psychological benefits. This innovative concept has been widely accepted all over the world.

Being a medical doctor born into a farmers family Dr Kataria found he was getting stressed out and he found relief in finding a fantastic tool to relieve the stress. He was also editing a health magazine at the same time which was also very stressful. Then on 13th March 1995 he discovered Laughter Yoga which totally changed his life. Soon he started inventing different exercises where people felt very good. Yet he realised he couldn't fake laughter for 30 seconds as within 30 seconds people started laughing for real and then it became infectious. He then blended this with yogic wisdom of India which is (PRANAYAMA) deep breathing exercises. Laughter itself is a breathing exercise because when you are laughing you are exhaling longer and it gets rid of toxic carbon dioxide which increases the oxygen supplied to your organs and brain which means you then become healthy with more energy. So you laugh for no reason and you laugh longer because natural laughter does not last for more than 3-4 seconds at a time and that doesn't bring health benefits. People have always talked about the benefits of laughter but what kind of laughter was beneficial? no-one really had any idea and it was then Dr Kataria found a breakthrough.

Laughter is beneficial only if you laugh long and heartily from the diaphragm which is belly laughter. So he called this Laughter Yoga.

Dr Kataria then stated that the world's number one sickness is Depression, Number 2 is Heart Disease and Number 3 is Cancer which are the major killers all over the world. He then stated that he'd not had a cough or cold for the past 20 years and at the laughter clubs he runs people do not fall sick. Also laughter eases pain because it releases endorphins and reduces pain by 50% straight away.

Dr Kataria stated that everybody in the world wants two things in their lives, to be happy and to be healthy. These two things are very illusive as many people are not happy today yet one exercise that can give people both health and happiness easily using exercise with little effort is Laughter Yoga. You have to realise that you may not get everything you want in life so it's better to be happy within yourself.

All over Governments are spending billions of dollars on health but they don't realise that by laughing 10-15 minutes a day you can be healthy because one of the best choices people can make is that laughter because it is the best medicine. The greatest part of Laughter Yoga is it combines the whole world as a family because laughter has no language. You are telling jokes and laughing without a reason. Everyone can learn and laugh in groups which is much easier and is a short cut to health and happiness and cost effective. You don't have to go to the Pharmacy because it's free of charge.

TOOLS, TIPS AND RECOMMENDATIONS

- In order to get the scientifically proven health benefits of laughter, we need to laugh continuously for at least for 10 to 15 minutes. Since in Laughter Yoga we do laughter as an exercise, we can prolong our laughter as long as we want. On the other hand, natural laughter comes for just a few seconds here and there and is not enough to bring about physiological and biochemical changes in our body.

- To reap the health benefits of laughter, laughter has to be loud and deep coming from the diaphragm. It should be a belly laugh. It might not be socially acceptable to laugh loudly, but Laughter Yoga clubs provide a safe environment where one can laugh loudly and heartily without any social implication.

- Natural laughter that courses through our life depends upon many reasons and conditions, but there are not many reasons which make us laugh. That means we are leaving laughter to chance, it may happen it may not. In contrast, in Laughter Yoga club we are not leaving laughter to chance, but doing it out of commitment. This is a guaranteed way of getting the health benefits of laughter.

Dr. Madan Kataria Founder Laughter Yoga Movement
http://www.laughteryoga.org/english

CHAPTER FIFTEEN – THE EFFECT OF FOOD ON OUR EMOTIONS

You are what you eat. Nutrition and health are definitely related. Think about it this way like a finely tuned car, your body needs the right fuel and regular maintenance (exercise, lifestyle and mental attitude) to achieve true health potential. If you put the wrong fuel in or let it go without regular use, there is no way it can deliver its full power and performance and you will get sick.

Maintaining a balanced diet can give you vitality, energy, help you stay at the right weight, boost your immune system, delay the effects of ageing, help with tiredness and fatigue, enhance the ability to ward off serious illnesses, enhances ability to concentrate and helps maintain blood sugar levels which affects mood swings.

Yet many people still do not associate behaviour and emotions with food and how it affects our emotions and so for me, this was another important aspect I wanted to feature in the book.

It can be difficult knowing where to start with diet and nutrition and what affects us and how it affects us, yet the more I follow my own journey with food and realise the effects it has on my body, mood and general well-being is the more I am making more conscious choices because my health is my wealth and that is important for me. Also due to the nature of the work I do and from many of the clients I see with series of illness or dis-ease this has made me even more aware of the huge part and importance food plays on our emotions.

Therefore, to get further insight into this important topic I spoke in brief with world renowned Health expert David Wolf and then subsequently interviewed Chef Dave Choi, who believes in plant based foods and Alison Henry, Health and Nutrition Consultant and Live Blood Specialist and this is what they shared about foods and emotions.

PART I

Esther: What do you think is the importance of food on emotions?

David: There is a very strong correlation between food and emotions. For example raw food has a happier energy to it. It's easier to yield higher vibrational emotions. When you're eating raw food or even when you're around raw food the colours of raw food and the brilliance of their colours and of super-foods is something that can impact your health. For example, yellow foods are associated with happiness, orange foods are associated with happiness. There is a connection between the brilliance of the colours and the emotional state that is associated with them. But when we start getting into the cooking of the food this definitely lowers the emotional vibration. The food looses its happy state to some degree and so this is why I have been such an advocate for raw food over the years because of its natural state of happiness and so there has to be some raw food in your diet in order to tap into those high energy emotions we all want to be feeling most of the time.

David Wolfe
Health, Eco, Nutrition, and Natural Beauty Expert

PART II

Chef Dave Choi is a retired vegan chef and creator of Just B Meditation and Healing Path. He has been teaching power of three deep breath and being/breathing in the moment with the mind, body, spirit which is related to air, water and food. So when you are grateful for everything on this planet earth everywhere can be a heaven.

Here Chef Choi talks about the link between food and our emotions.

Dave: For the purpose of your book, I would say that there are a lot of different ways of translating wounded. It could be physical, mindful or spiritual. We are living in this body with the mind, body and spirit trying to do different things and life can be harsh because when your mind, body and spirit are trying to do different things this is what is called "wounded" because it means you are not happy.

Esther: You are very mindful about the food you consume and the energy of that food in terms of healing, can you share more about what that means?

Dave: Right now I am involved in a documentary movie to be released March 2015. It's a two hour documentary called "Food Choice." Everything has its own soul. Every living creature has its own language, sound and movement. Human beings have this digestive system equivalent of a plant based engine. We have this long tube from the upper intestine to lower intestine which is designed to graze on plant based food. But we are putting all kinds of animal based protein that is stressed out into our body. We are then breaking this food down which creates an environment where there is lots of acidity in the body which creates all types of incurable diseases like cancer and all kinds of neurological disorders. I am a good friend of **Dr T. Colin Campbell** author of The China Study and he is a Research Doctor at the Cornell University, USA. He says that if a person eliminates sugar, yeast, meat protein and diary protein out of their diet they will never have to worry about getting cancer or any other kind of free radical cell development in the human body.

Do you know what is happening in Chicago at this moment? There is a shooting rampage every day. It's like the killing capital of the world. One of the biggest issues of this happening South Side of Chicago especially with African Americans is because people are eating a lot of emotional food. They enjoy a lot of sugar, spice, sodium and then they enjoy a lot of food that has carcinogens i.e barbecues etc and plus if you add things like alcohol, cigarettes and drugs the body becomes very hollow and then it becomes unable to think what's right and what's wrong.

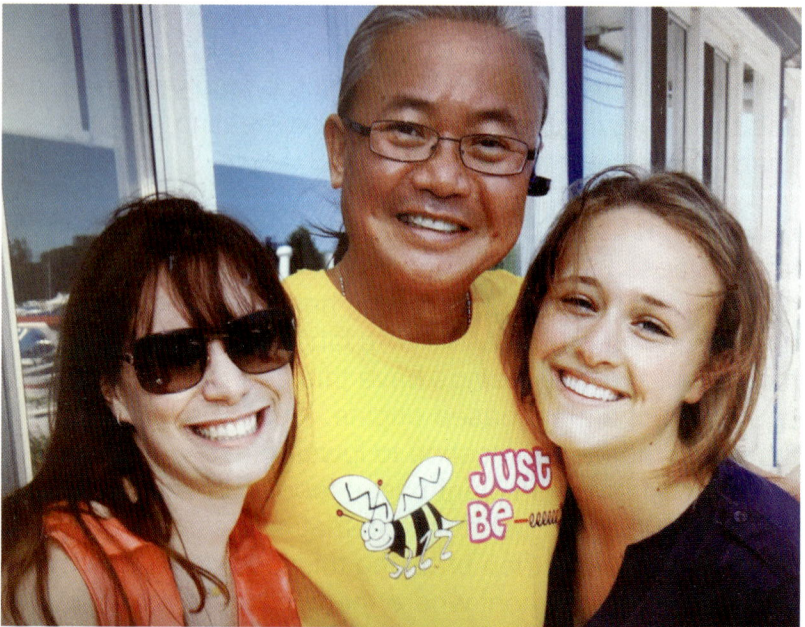

For example in a country like Japan if a person gets convicted in the prison system they eliminate all meat, diary and sugar out of their diet. Why? because if you eat plant based protein and a plant based diet without any kind of stimulate the mind becomes calm. During the horrific Japanese earth quake and Tsunami there was a maximum penitentiary near the prison and all the prisoner's had every opportunity to escape but they decided to stay in prison and came down to help the citizens in the area. This just goes to show what food does in the decision making process and beyond.

Esther: What else can you tell us about Wounds and food and emotions in order to empower people to deal with their emotional baggage?

Dave: It's all about love. If you start your day with love that means you go through your whole day with love turning negatives to positives. You cannot control your own destiny whilst you are sleeping because that is the only time when you have "died" in your sleep. – It's uncontrollable destiny. So it's about saying farewell to yourself before you go to bed hoping to see yourself the next day and when you rise in the morning you resurrect from the dead. Look at yourself in the mirror and award yourself and tell yourself "I love you." If you do that your life becomes much simpler because in order to love someone else you have to establish a basic relationship with your mind, body and spirit to be in one harmonious way in the name of love.

Chef Dave Choi
Founder Just Bee Meditation and Healing Paths - Just Bee Life Breathe Meditation Founder & Medicinal Vegan Buddhist Chef, Energy Healer

FOOD AND EMOTIONS – PART III

Esther: What are your thoughts on the topic of Wounded Lives, Wounded Healers in terms of how it affects us and our health?

Alison: It's very detrimental to health first and foremost. It's important to understand what is holding one back in terms of spiritual and physical development and overall being healthy. So in terms of problems from the past your body holds onto illness and does not promote wellness and this can have a profound effect on the endocrine system and lead to hormone imbalances.

Esther: Can you further expand on the statement around our hormones?

Alison: Our adrenal glands are the organs which deal with stress. This is associated with the way our body uses insulin. The relationship between the adrenal glands and insulin is if you are stressed all the time you are giving out cortisol.

When we are stressed it has huge impact on the adrenal glands this also has an impact on the way our body uses insulin.

When you are stressed when you worry and when you are carrying emotional baggage associated with stress, this has an impact on our blood sugar. The reason for this is that stress requires energy and the body needs energy to process sugar. Stress equals more sugar demands in the blood. Stress means the adrenal glands are working harder where the adrenal glands should work in fight or flight state which is how they should be working in a normal state. It helps us to respond to things we perceive as danger. So when we are worrying and carrying stress all the time, we are in the flight or fight state all the time. In a run, run mode all the time.

Another aspect of how food impacts on our emotions. From the very start of your life you develop a deep association linking food to reward and pleasure; from which the by products are your emotions. As babies and infants your cries are rewarded with food, as you move through life you continue to link food to emotional rewards, example of this are weddings, promotions, graduations and birthdays to name a few so therefore food is also used to support emotions in love.

Your brain is responsible for reward and pleasure; your brain's neuro transmitter such as Dopamine, Norepinephrine and Serotonin has various effects on your behaviour patterns which stems from how you feel, based on what you see, hear, eat or think. From a food and emotion perspective your Dopamine and Norepinephrine need protein such as lentils, beans, quinoa, spinach, fish and eggs. The later needs carbohydrates such as whole wheat, brown rice, fruits and vegetables, plantain, pineapple, kiwi, plums and tomatoes.

Unhealthy foods can interfere with your neuro transmitter natural flow and this can result in chemical imbalances which can change the way you feel. Craving foods is a sign of nutritional imbalances. After you eat the food that you crave you feel better or happier, this is reflected by your emotions and in your behaviour.

TOOLS, TIPS AND RECOMMENDATIONS

- Healthy fats such as omega 3, 6 and 9 found in fish, olives, coconut oil and vegetable oil are necessary as they support brain function and hormone balancing and thus better emotions. Fatty acid DHA, docosahexaenoic acid is the most abundant fat found in the brain.

- Water is important for good blood flow, waste removal and hydration, low water intake can affect the way you look and feel.

- Exercise is vital, a natural feel good factor it encourages the release of adrenalin and you feel more energy and so you feel better about yourself.

- For a food perspective natural healthy foods are much better for your overall health as they can help you to stay in control and therefore manage your emotions by what you choose to eat and thereby avoid emotional cycles which are easily adopted.

Alison Henry
Health Nutrition Consultant and Live Blood Specialist
Private Healing Clinic, Harley Street, London

CHAPTER 16 – FROM THE BRINK OF DEATH TO A BEACON OF LIGHT

Dr Linda Salvin is someone who has survived 3 near death experiences in the '80s. A series of devastating accidents transformed her life. Linda survived a commercial airliner crash in 1981. As she was sliding down the shoot, Linda had an out-of-body experience. That was the beginning of her psychic and spiritual transformation. A year later, she was struck by a fire truck and in 1984, another traumatic auto accident brought her to the white light. Surgery in 1991 proved to be another life-altering experience, opening her healing gifts and by 1996, her body developed tumours from healing she performed on others which needed to be removed. After the first of three surgeries for the tumours, Linda became a transmedium and began communicating with the other side to assist other people. With each of these experiences, her spiritual connection, psychic, healing and mediumship abilities grew Yet rather than dwell on her own challenges, Linda reached out to further assist and heal others.

Linda explains that the more we experience on the human level pain, grief, guilt, shame, loss, excitement and love - all the different emotions and situations whether career, love life, sex life, family life, romantic life or travel whatever we are doing – there is always someone who comes to us who has a similar question or experience, by giving and expressing themselves to us in order to find comfort and for us to tell them they are not alone on this journey. This is also amplified by the fact that as well as having the gift of insight, intuition and psychic abilities this gives them more guidance and insight which acts as some type of pacifier at that time. Whatever we are doing and experience, there is always someone who comes to us because of who we are.

After the Boeing 737 plane crash where the plane crash landed and the engine fell off, the landing gear was stripped and the plane cracked in half upon impact. I ran out on the field and when I stopped, it was as if I were 50 feet out of my body on the left and standing 5'8" on the right. I'd had an out-of-body experience and I became a walk in. It was a result of this accident that I became very psychic. But because this was all new to me it was very daunting because the fear of getting up, spending time alone, getting messages I had never heard before made it a very anxiety ridden time. I was in therapy for a long time and it was a very confusing and painful decade for me. I was 27 at the time of the plane crash and 28 when the fire truck hit my car at which time I had another out of body experience. I had post traumatic stress and didn't want to leave my apartment. There was so much trauma that I absorbed and I couldn't manage it. Then in 1984 during a rainstorm, I totalled my car in an accident. As I was spinning out, I saw the white light. The beam went from my head into the ceiling of my car and into the heavens. The same voice that spoke to me during the plane crash spoke again, giving me a choice to live or die. I obviously stayed but the spiritual awakening increased even more as did my fears. I had no idea what was happening to me back then. It was one traumatic event after another. It was too much for anyone to handle.

This was a very frightening and difficult time for me. Especially dealing with fear and being sensitive because as you know we are used to everything being so bright so when the darkness comes it's even more overwhelming; it's like a deep well.

So your book is about how to get over the negativity and the pain. For me I have dealt with my traumas through Meditation, prayer and through talking to God. Also helping other human beings helps to take the focus off me and to trust that the Universe knows more than I do, because if I know that God or the Universe is in control then I really am not in control. It's my Will verses God's Will which are two totally different things. A lot of the anxiety goes away and the darkness lightens up. It's the patience to walk through the tragedy, the trauma and to talk about it and to tell people where I am at. That is the hardest part of being a healer, people don't want to know I have an issue but I am only human.

For me, there are times I know I hold onto certain things from the past or I remember something and it becomes an obsession. Then there are months that go by and I don't even think about the past, because I'm so much in the moment doing my work that I do not have time for emotional baggage. But when it does hit me I will write and journal or I'll talk to someone. I pray a lot. Sometimes I light candles of which I have a line called "Wicks of Wisdom." I think there are different techniques for everyone. Some people are clinically disturbed or hurt or depressed that require professional help from a medical doctor. Others can have emotional differences and it's about how to recognise what the baggage is rather than the reality.

There are times I would think about a man I rejected for marriage. I wasn't ready. It was after the plane crash and the fire truck accident. I was more than stressed due to the confusion and pain I was in. This man was pursuing me yet I felt I could not be in a relationship. I'm just wasn't ready and asked why did God do this? But if I had been more honest and open with him I would've told him that I was going through a difficult time and to be patient with me. I was intimidated by him because he was everything I wanted/dreamed off and I rejected him and sometimes I go back to "we could've had children, we could've travelled etc" who knows? Hindsight always speaks louder than the moment. We make decisions and then we go back and wish it had been different or that we should've taken this road or that road or made different decisions and then we end up where we are. The biggest key is acceptance in the moment. We have to accept where we are and who we are, what we are doing and if we want to change the future we have to change ourselves and take that first step towards a new beginning in the moment.

TOOLS, TIPS AND RECOMMENDATIONS

- Like everyone I have different truths and like you I have to practice what I preach.

- Everything happens for a reason and sometimes we can't see that and we are stuck in the middle of the malaise – but if you pray and have faith it will work out and it's usually only a temporary set-back.

Dr Linda Salvin, MPH, PhD
Talk Show Host
Metaphysician
http://www.lindasalvin.com

RESOURCES BY ESTHER AUSTIN

Can be purchased at Amazon, www.authorhouse.co.uk, www.estheraustinglobal.com

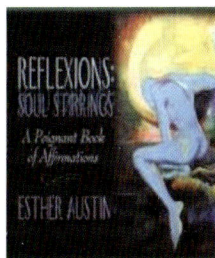

Reflexions Soul Stirrings is a powerful book of affirmations, positive and heart-warming insight which seeks to uplift, heal, inspire and empower.

ISBN: 9781434312129

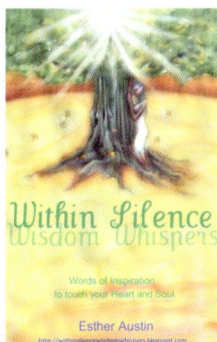

Within Silence, Wisdom Whispers weaves a creative and powerful insight into life. The book aims to be a blueprint for those who are on a personal development journey looking to find their inner truth.

ISBN-10: 1908341785
ISBN 13: 978-1908341785

http://www. withinsilencewisdomwhispers.blogspot.co.uk/

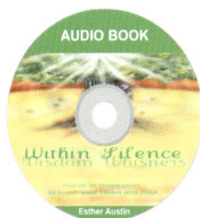

Within Silence, Wisdom Whispers Audiobook

ISBN: 978-0-9545918-2-3

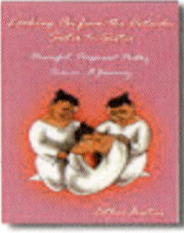

Looking on from the Outside: Sister to Sister is a selection of poetry about the emotional roller coaster experienced by my family as my younger sister was diagnosed with cancer. It journeys through pain, grief, futility, hope and the struggle to comprehend circumstances around this disease.

ISBN: 9781425937294

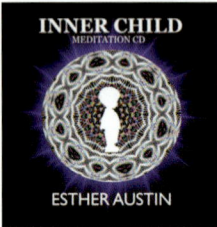

A powerful yet gentle meditation CD which takes you on a journey to connect with your inner child in order to find whatever you are searching for whether that be peace, clarity, forgiveness, love, understanding.

ISBN: 978-0-954 5918-5-4

Details can be found at www.estheraustinglobal.com
Meditation Cover Designed by Cameron Austin-Buah

Recommended Resources and Services

Astric Rausch from Divinity's Divine Touch comes highly recommended by myself. She is a gifted Intuitive Reader and Healer. She is able to offer in-depth spiritual guidance and readings giving you an insight into your life whilst offering guidance on a way forward. Astric has a very gentle and caring way of delivering her readings and you will walk away enlightened, empowered and with clarity.

www.etsy.com/shop/divinitysdivinetouch

Meditation by Bob Proctor

'Calmness of mind is one of the beautiful jewels of wisdom.' – James Allen

We've all heard the incredible benefits of meditation and relaxation – now you can be guided through a personalized meditation with the world's foremost authority on success, Bob Proctor.

Get your complimentary, personalized relaxation audio here: www.RelaxWithBob.com and reap the benefits of relaxing into results.

Esther Austin
International Intuitive Healer

Transforming,

Empowering and

Healing Lives

✔ Hypno-Analysis and Regression Therapist
✔ Intuitive Reader
✔ African Healing Dance Practitioner
✔ Bach Flower Remedy Consultant
✔ Intuitive Personal Coach
✔ Equine and Animal Healer & Communicator

info@estheraustinglobal.com | www.estheraustinglobal.com | 07534 508919

Designing Access

My Mission
Bringing High Functioning Adults
Relationship Success through Emotional Education and Development
with Conscious Tools, Structures and Practices
for Becoming an Emotionally Mature, Spiritual Adult.

Projects and Services I Offer Clients

Conscious Dating Creating Your Soul-Mate Relationship
Pre-Marital Project
Conscious Couples Relationships
Life Purpose; Creating Life's Work
Foundations for Small Business Partnerships
Shamanic Ceremonies
Equine Assisted Courses: FEEL through HorseJourneys

Special Offer

$100 off Your First Month
Consulting with Cindy Jarrett

I offer a non-fee consultation ranging from 1.1/2 to 2 hours
for all prospective clients to determine what they require
and for all potential clients to discover
the depth of my services.

I work by phone, in person & by Skype -
all time zones covered!

(707) 824 – 8474

www.HorseJourneys.com   www.DesigningAccess.biz

ACKNOWLEDGEMENTS

To everyone I interviewed or who contributed to this book in some way, Dr Chef Dave Choi, Alison Henry, David Wolfe, Jackee Holder, Cindy Jarrett, Devi Ward, James D'Angelou, Lyz Cooper, Wyoma, Patricia Cori, Dr Katari, Mavis Amankwah, Gayle Edwards, Grace Ononiwu, Dr Linda Salvin, thank you all for sharing, for your honesty, time and commitment to working with me on this book.

To my two boys Cameron and Ashley – thank you for being who you are. You have both empowered me to step more into who I am through the reflections of our relationships. My love for you both has inspired me to hold onto my dreams and purpose. Also giving thanks to my beautiful new grand-daughter Mia Bella and her beautiful mother Annabel Ifil, Cameron – you are a lucky man.

To a wonderful man, confidant, friend, soul-mate Kenneth Barrett. Your presence in my life allows me to recognise the expansiveness of true love and to not be afraid to share it and to have patience with life at times.

To Justin and Millie Lewis for loving me as a daughter and standing unconditionally by my side and affirming my journey through words of encouragement.

To Lubna and Rehan Ul Haq –thank you both always for your unconditional love and dedicated belief in me for more than 20 years.

To Owen-Alexander-Ffrench, my adopted big brother – thank you so much for your constant encouragement and unconditional love and our times of laughter.

To Sister Abbaanah for her laughter and encouragement and great in-depth discussions about life

ABOUT

Esther Austin is a gifted International Intuitive Healer and runs her own Healing Practice with her partner. Esther is best described as a Balance Practitioner because she establishes balance back into YOUR life. You already have balance within you. Yet sometimes unbalance occurs due to painful emotional, physical and psychological situations which are never addressed nor resolved.

Therefore, Esther has the Keys to Unlock your emotional pain by using a range of powerful healing and transformational modalities which support you back into wholeness and back into YOUR balance.

Qarma Therapies: Esther has devised various well-being healing packages to suit a client's needs and she runs Holistic Healing Retreats with her partner in some of the most beautiful locations around the world.

Qarma Broadcast: Esther is a Radio Presenter and Broadcaster. Esther set up Qarma Broadcast www.qarmabroadcast.co.uk in 2007 to honor her late sister Deborah. She now runs the station with her partner. Qarma Broadcast's ethos is about transforming, empowering and healing lives. The station covers shows about health and nutrition, healing, well-being, personal transformation and much more.

Contact: info@estheraustinglobal.com
Website: www.estheraustinglobal.com

AFTERWORD

I have had one of the most amazing journeys writing this book. It has been challenging to a certain degree but I have learned so much along the way. I now have a better understanding about a wider range of healing modalities. I also feel so blessed for the time each individual who contributed to this book took to talk and share with me about their work and their lives as well as giving me time to interview them. More profoundly for me they all shared from a deep place of honesty, integrity and authenticity which weaved and created the powerful information you've read in this book.

Through what has been shared, I too have grown. I have laughed, I have felt my heart pour out, I have been enlightened. I have been forced to look at my own life and my own way of being at times and have had to adjust so I could further stand in my truth, authenticity and power. Throughout this process I have shed many skins and as a result I feel so much stronger within who I am, at this moment in time, for all the precious nuggets of wisdom that was shared.

So wherever you are at in your life, whatever you are experiencing, if you have journeyed through this book and someones experience of healing has touched you why not get in touch with them. Think about starting your journey into wholeness TODAY. Gift yourself a chance to transform and embrace a new way of living and being. Gift yourself the chance to finally set yourself free.

To Shirley Ann-Hunte who has stood by my side supporting me with building my dream and always with a smile and a "what do you need.

To God who has given me passion and purpose to reach out and serve humanity in whatever way I am guided. To my ancestors i.e my late mother, father, sister Deborah, Auntie Pearl and all those who stand strong behind me – thank you for I hold onto your strength always and wisdom.